Original title:
What Is Life, But a Series of Google Searches?

Copyright © 2025 Creative Arts Management OÜ
All rights reserved.

Author: Dorian Ashford
ISBN HARDBACK: 978-1-80566-124-5
ISBN PAPERBACK: 978-1-80566-419-2

Queries in the Cosmos

Why is the sky so blue today?
Do cats dream of fish in play?
Can squirrels ride bikes on the trees?
Is cheese just a form of tease?

What's the best way to cook a shoe?
Can I gain strength from a bowl of stew?
Why do fruit flies look so keen?
Is a cactus a porcupine in green?

If I eat cake, will I turn it sweet?
Can you teach a goldfish to tweet?
Do ghosts like to dance in the night?
Is my Wi-Fi just out of sight?

Is time a flat circle, they say?
Can I order pizza for today?
What's the secret to happiness here?
Is laughter just chocolate, my dear?

The Search Engine of Existence

How to nap through a boring lecture?
Can a sandwich truly be a vector?
Do clouds have meetings in the air?
Will socks forever disappear?

Is it true that cats plot our fate?
What do unicorns eat on a plate?
Can spaghetti dance with a tune?
Are we all just lost in a balloon?

Why do we love cheesy dad jokes?
Can a vacuum cleaner take a poke?
Is a pillow a portable cloud?
Will my fish ever join a crowd?

If a tree falls, does it clap its hands?
Can I understand life's loose strands?
How to keep my plants truly alive?
Is Google the reason we strive?

Web Pages and Wistfulness

If a meme is serious, is it still funny?
Can we find joy in anything sunny?
What's the secret behind the art?
Is Wi-Fi love just a clever start?

Can penguins wish upon a star?
Why does my phone have a memory bar?
Is a bruise a badge of honor worn?
Do millennials feel forever torn?

When does a Google frog become a prince?
Can a sandwich dare to give me hints?
How to tell if my cake is moist?
Is my plant now my inner voice?

What's the recipe for bliss and cheer?
Why is laundry never quite clear?
Can I search for happiness and thrive?
Is the key to existence just being alive?

Unraveling Existence

If life's a puzzle, where's the piece?
Can I summon joy with some good cheese?
What's the best way to lose my keys?
Why do I laugh at dad's old knees?

Do llamas make friends with the moon?
Can I sing a tune to my vacuum?
How to find socks lost in the wash?
Do jellybeans always make me posh?

If I pray to Google, will it respond?
Can pasta really make me fond?
How to eat dessert before my meal?
Is that spinning chair really a wheel?

Are puns the essence of our fate?
Can a potato hold the weight?
What's the secret to making it rain?
Is joy just a click away, I gain?

Keywords and Curiosities

In the search bar I dwell,
Typing questions so swell.
Why do socks go missing?
Can potatoes really sing?

Puffed queries blend and twist,
Like a plot that can't be missed.
How to charm a squirrel?
Is coffee a magic whirl?

Lost in a sea of "how to,"
Searching for the bright and new.
Can cats play the piano?
What's up with that big rhino?

Each click brings chuckles and glee,
Another odd thought spree.
What snacks go well with wine?
Do robots dream? That's divine!

In Pursuit of Pixelated Truths

I'm in a quest every night,
For knowledge, a digital flight.
What's the secret to a pie?
Can a cactus say goodbye?

Scrolling through the funny memes,
Chasing down bizarre dreams.
How to dance like a pro?
Can I juggle flaming dough?

Endless links and wild tales,
What's with the internet snails?
Checked if cheese can come alive,
What if squirrels could drive?

From silly pranks to wild facts,
In this web, nothing lacks.
Do unicorns really trot?
Can I win the pie-eating lot?

Collective Queries of the Heart

We gather questions like stars,
In a galaxy of bizarre.
How to woo a pizza slice?
Can spaghetti roll the dice?

What does love taste like today?
Is it cookies? Or a bouquet?
How to befriend a broom?
Can a mirror hold a gloom?

Searches link us, every part,
Questions are a form of art.
Can I train my pet goldfish?
Should I wish or just not wish?

Through pixels, hearts collide,
In giggles, we must confide.
What if clouds wear silly hats?
Do we talk to our pet cats?

The Algorithm of Desire

In the feed of endless scroll,
Hunting down my heart and soul.
What's the best way to eat cake?
Can I bake a giant snake?

Algorithms know my whims,
Recommending dance and hymns.
How to train a wild llama?
What's a life without drama?

Searching for joy in small things,
Like how butterflies have wings.
Do plants prefer a sweet tune?
Are stars just dreams in a balloon?

Each click opens funny doors,
With laughter, my spirit soars.
What if ice cream could fly?
Can I teach a frog to sigh?

Unraveling Queries

Each click a question, a spark of light,
Pondering cats that can play the night.
Whispers of wisdom found in a byte,
Chasing down answers, like a kite in flight.

Recipes for dinners, and how to dance,
What's the best way to cook a steak, perchance?
And why does my phone ring when I glance?
Life feels like weird, digital romance.

From memes to dreams, the data flows,
Why does my coffee taste like memories?
Each query a puzzle, where nonsense grows,
In a web of laughter, life's mysteries.

With every search, a rabbit hole deep,
How to make friends, how to lose sleep?
A digital circus, oh what a leap,
Inquiries funny, thoughts to keep.

Digital Dreams

Floating through screens, in a pixel cheer,
Asking my phone, 'What do I hold dear?'
Searching for snacks and the latest meme,
A digital wonderland, chasing a dream.

In a world of bytes, I question my fate,
Can dogs wear pants, or is that just great?
Why does my computer hold secrets so tight?
And how do we know that aliens are right?

Each click a laugh, a giggle unleashed,
From cat videos, I find joy increased.
How to fold laundry? Send that to space!
The queries grow wilder, what a mad race!

In this realm of light, I find pure glee,
Searching for wisdom, just me and my PC.
Digital laughter, a humorous spree,
What else can I find? Oh, just wait and see!

Searching for Serenity

Tap, tap, tap, what brings me peace?
Can I find zen with a Google piece?
How to breathe easy, let worries slide,
In this whirlwind search, I take a ride.

From yoga poses to smoothies divine,
Is there a recipe for a calmer mind?
How to relax in a world so fast?
Sometimes I wonder, can calm really last?

Do fish get stressed? I ponder and muse,
What's the right method to choose my shoes?
Is there a button to stop all the fuss?
Searching for calm in this digital rush.

With each typed word, I seek out the light,
How to find joy without a fight?
Can I download peace? Is there an app?
In this search for joy, I take a nap!

Echoing Emotions

In cyberspace, feelings get a voice,
'Help me feel calm, oh sweet search choice.'
Why am I sad? A text on the screen,
Explore each emotion, what does it mean?

Searching for laughter, quick-fix delight,
Can emojis ease a lonely night?
Where's the link for a heart, full and bright?
In a web of queries, I find my light.

Why do I cringe at my old high school hair?
Longing for moments that weren't always fair.
Do dogs really care when I'm feeling blue?
Turns out they love me, my search said it too!

Google's my friend, my personal guide,
Asking the cosmos where giggles abide.
In these echoing searches, emotions collide,
Digital heartbeats, I'm taking this ride!

Browser Windows to the Soul

In a world of tabs, I roam and scroll,
Each click a thought, each search a goal.
Searching for answers with a flick and a swipe,
Google, my friend, you're my online type.

A query for pizza, I hunt for my snack,
But soon I'm lost in a meme-filled track.
How to fix life? I type with glee,
But the results just show cats up a tree.

At midnight I ponder, 'Am I alone?'
Yet here I am, in a digital zone.
Searching for dreams, how to be wise,
But I end up with videos of guys in ties.

So here's to the browsers and all their charms,
Their windows reflect a world full of harms.
In laughter, we find the answers we seek,
In search bars and links, we'll never feel weak.

Seeking Through Screens

I type in my woes, hoping for aid,
Instead I get pop-ups that seem to invade.
'Why do socks disappear in the wash?' I want to know,
And end up learning about the stars that glow.

How to have fun, or how to unwind,
Google suggests I leave my troubles behind.
Searching for meaning in fluffy cat gifs,
My heart finds joy in these unconventional lifts.

I seek self-improvement, or the perfect roast,
But stumble on facts that scare me the most.
YouTube tutorials, a rabbit hole wide,
I start with a dream, and end up mystified.

Through screens I wander, seeking and lost,
With every new search a laugh at the cost.
In the web's absurdity, I find some grace,
Clicking away, I quicken the pace.

Keywords of the Heart

Love and romance, I search and explore,
But find lists of dating tips galore.
How to woo someone, or how to flirt,
But all I gain is a dessert recipe alert.

I type in my feelings, my heart all afire,
Get links to manage a stress-filled choir.
How to express, what words should I jot?
But it's dog videos that I've clicked and forgot.

Life hacks and wonders, what gives me delight?
The secrets of life, in the glow of the night.
While seeking the truth, I laugh and I smile,
Life's most profound lessons take me a while.

In pixels and bytes, I find what I crave,
Between searches for wisdom, a world misbehaves.
With laughs in my heart, I take a deep breath,
And click on the memes that conquer the stress.

The Infinite Search

Endless queries to fill the void,
In a search machine, I'm overjoyed.
'How to bake bread?' or 'How to relax?'
But end up with lists on vintage knick-knacks.

Each question I type unfurls a new thread,
A voyage where common sense seems to shred.
I lose track of time, awash in delight,
As I navigate nonsense that glows in the night.

Wonder and whimsy in every new seek,
Yet, why does my plant look so very bleak?
I look for solutions, and sometimes a laugh,
While stumbling on websites that make me feel daft.

So here's to the search, the endless pursuit,
In the dance of the clicks, my woes take a boot.
With humor and joy, I'll never despair,
In this boundless quest, I find what I share.

Pixels of Perception

In a world of clicks and scrolls,
We find ourselves in endless holes.
Searching for the meaning, we dare,
Only to find cat memes everywhere.

What's the cure for a bad hair day?
A how-to guide or a cab ride away?
With each search, we hope to discover,
The secrets of life—like a pizza delivery cover!

Life hacks promise to make us wise,
But often lead to silly surprise.
In the pixels of our frantic quest,
We find we're just like all the rest.

From Googling dreams to pie recipes,
We scan the web with digital ease.
Existence seems like a playful jest,
A web of wonders that never lets us rest.

The Browser of Being

Open a tab, what's on today?
Life advice or a quick buffet?
In a browser of being, we swipe and scroll,
Trying to figure out our own role.

Searching for wisdom, we get distracted,
By videos of dogs who are very enacted.
And while we ponder the meaning of fate,
We find ourselves lost in a meme state.

FAQs promise the answers we seek,
Yet lead us down a pathway oblique.
With every query, we question our worth,
Finding depth in a GIF's moment of mirth.

Clicks of Curiosity

With every click, a new thread to pull,
Curiosity piqued, isn't it beautiful?
Searching for answers in endless pages,
Learning, laughing, through the digital stages.

'How to cook pasta' or 'How to dance?'
Each question a chance for a whimsical chance.
In this endless scroll, we chuckle and tease,
As life feels like a game of mind-twisting fees.

From how to tame our messy hair,
To thoughts on quantum mechanics laid bare,
We wander through pixels, questions in tow,
Finding humor in every mishap that we sow.

Inputting Our Existence

Typing away, I ponder it all,
In search of answers, I may take a fall.
Is there a cheat code for this daily grind?
Or a guide to happiness carefully designed?

With each keystroke, I hit and miss,
Digging for meaning I thought I'd find bliss.
The quantum of questions makes me chuckle,
As I click on a link, my brain starts to buckle.

Have I found answers or just more strife?
In the chaos of queries, I search for life.
And amidst all the nonsense, I choose to laugh,
For in this grand search, I'm just part of the graph.

Dialectics of Digital Discovery

A click for answers, oh what a mess,
From cat videos to existential stress.
In the vast web, my thoughts do roam,
Searching for meaning, I find a meme home.

In the search bar, I type 'how to be wise',
But all I find are makeup tips and fries.
Life's grand questions with quick fingertips,
Translate to GIFs and sweet potato clips.

I ponder deep thoughts, hit enter, and wait,
Suggested results say 'date your fate'.
Algorithms know me better than I know,
For life's quirky answers, my browser's a pro.

So here I sit, with snacks piled high,
Searching for wisdom, while cats pass by.
In the digital maze, I find my delight,
The comedy of life, in each search I write.

The Cyberspace Chronicles

Click, click, and scroll, what do I see?
A video of squirrels chasing a bee.
In this grand saga of online delight,
I search for enlightenment, and end up with bites.

The more I ponder, the more I lose track,
Searching for answers, then back to the snacks.
From 'how to adult' to 'best pizza place',
Life's little mysteries turn into a race.

Each search reveals a new rabbit hole,
Mind blown by trivia, that's out of control.
'How to speak whale?' and 'wearing socks with crocs?'
Turns out my wisdom is in paradox socks.

In this cyberspace tale, where I roam so free,
I find joy in the silly, that's my decree.
With laughter and memes, I'll face the unknown,
The chronicles of searching are whimsically grown.

The URL of Existence

Life's a URL, just click and explore,
From deep thoughts to snacks, there's always more.
I query my soul, and guess what I find?
Links to recipes that boggle the mind.

Thought I was searching for wisdom and grace,
But all I uncover's a dance how-to base.
The essence of being feels lost in the stream,
Yet somehow I'd rather just binge-watch a meme.

Typing away, with coffee in hand,
I dive into topics both silly and grand.
What's the meaning of life? Pick a search term,
Only to find out a cactus can squirm.

So here's to the clicks that keep life so spry,
To understand living before I can die.
With a chuckle I say, as I browse and scroll,
Every question's a journey that brightens the soul.

Uncharted URLs

In a sea of links and clicks,
I search for socks and cat pics.
With every query I unfold,
A tale of randomness, untold.

From recipes to how to bake,
My browser's history, what a quake!
A treasure trove of odd delights,
Each search revealing new insights.

I typed in 'how to dance like me',
But all I found was a funny bee.
Yet in this maze of endless scroll,
I find a spark that fills my soul.

So here's to all the clicks we'd make,
In digital realms, our hearts awake.
Navigating through this vast array,
Searching for laughs in our own way.

The Memory Cache of Existence

In the cache of my online life,
I seek advice to end my strife.
'How to fix a leaky tap?'
And end up lost in a meme trap.

Browsed through myths and legends bold,
Found a GIF of a dog, uncontrolled.
Every search a piece of fate,
In this chaos, I contemplate.

Forgotten passwords make me sweat,
But googling 'how to not forget?'
Leads to a guide on cooking fish,
A memory cache I wish to squish!

So here's to all the stored-up dreams,
And silly thoughts within the streams.
Each search a stitch in life's grand quilt,
In digital play, my fears are spilt.

Whispers in the Web

Whispers float on the web so wide,
Queries like whispers, I cannot hide.
'How to dance like no one watches?'
Yet my moves make all the bots scotches.

Got lost in forums, a rabbit hole,
Were those directions for a troll?
Each answer like a little greet,
From a stranger who's stuck in defeat.

Searched for wisdom, but found a cat,
Dressed as a pirate, imagine that!
In every search, a chuckle lies,
My heart cracks open, oh how time flies.

So I'll keep questioning every whim,
Letting the web pull me in on a limb.
With laughter echoing in each find,
In digital lands, I'm never blind.

Chronicles of Curiosity

Oh, the quests that I undertake,
For random facts and life's big break.
'Why do we sneeze?' I seek to know,
But end up with tweets from the show.

Searched for wisdom from the wise,
But all I found were pizza pies.
Each link a twist in my fate,
A funny charm I'll celebrate.

Questions spiral as I implore,
'How do I deal with an open door?'
But what comes next's an endless scroll,
My mind races, searching for a role.

In chronicles of curious quests,
I find the fun that never rests.
Every click a journey, taking flight,
In this digital dance, I feel so light.

A Timeline of Keywords

I typed in 'how to cook'
Google said 'easy' with a hook.
Then I searched 'why is my cat sad?'
Turns out she's just a little mad.

Next was 'DIY solar panel'
Lost three hours, but felt quite grand.
'Best late-night snacks to munch?'
Cheese puffs, pizza, why not a bunch?

And who could forget that day?
'How to dance like Beyoncé?'
The results were not what I'd hope,
Two left feet, can't even cope.

So many questions mark my path,
Each search returns a little laugh.
As I scroll through this vast array,
I wonder what I'll type today.

The Web of Wonder

A search for 'funny cat memes'
Led me down the internet's streams.
But suddenly I lost my way,
Found a quiz: 'Which cat are you today?'

'How to flirt with a crush,' I ask,
Every article feels like a task.
'Is my crush into me?' I plead,
The answers vary, I'm filled with greed.

Then I find myself in deep,
Researching why my plants won't leap.
What's wrong with my poor fern?
'Plant parenting': twist and turn.

Each click a chance for a new delight,
A browser window open all night.
The web spins tales and funny finds,
With questions that occupy my mind.

Inquiries of the Heart

I googled 'how to get over him,'
Found tips, but the light grew dim.
'What do I do with my ex's shoes?'
Google smiled, suggested: 'Donate or snooze.'

Next search, 'how to be more bold,'
Got advice that never grows old.
'Steal his hoodie,' the internet said,
That might just bring comfort instead.

Then 'how to cook for a date?'
Burned the pasta, not so great.
But when I looked into his eyes,
Life's little blunders felt like a prize.

Through every quest and heartfelt sigh,
Just typing on a whim to get by.
For love's a series of clicks and taps,
In this wild adventure, my heart perhaps.

The Infinite Scroll

Scrolling through life, one page at a time,
Each search engine feels like a rhyme.
'How to nap like a pro,' I find,
Comfy positions, the sweet unwind.

'How to get rich without a plan?'
Most hits just said, 'become a fan.'
And as I read with a skeptical grin,
The ads for fast cash can't help but spin.

Then came a query, 'best travel hacks,'
All places away, packed with snack packs.
Clicked 'buy tickets for cheap flights,' oh boy,
Only to find the deals are a ploy.

Every keyword opens a door,
To silly insights and memes galore.
In this vast ocean of fun-filled prose,
I giggle as life offers humorous throws.

Serendipity in Search

In the quiet night, I query cats,
Searching best pizza, or where's my hat?
Lost in the web, a rabbit hole spins,
Found a meme that made my day begin.

For every question, there's just one friend,
The wise old Google, always to lend.
I type with glee, my worries I cast,
Life's little mysteries, they zoom by fast.

From DIY crafts to how to cook roast,
I'm laughing aloud with my digital host.
Algorithms dance, with tricks up their sleeves,
Teaching me life with each joke it weaves.

So here's to the search—a delightful spree,
Unraveling chaos, setting my mind free.
With every click, I ride on a quest,
In this playful game, I find my zest.

The Syntax of Sentience

Life's just a code, a curious sting,
Searching for answers—does laughter bring?
I ask if squirrels ever have a plan,
And wonder who's faster, cat or the man?

Syntax of life, I query the muse,
What's the best way to tie my shoes?
Questions abound like stars in the sky,
With each little search, my giggles comply.

Is pizza edible at 3 AM?
Do llamas laugh when they see a gem?
Google suggests as I ponder and think,
A fountain of jokes, without any ink.

So let's not fret, but ask what we wish,
For wisdom is served in a digital dish.
In this playful world, with each search I beam,
Dancing with queries, life's a funny dream.

Google Grains of Wisdom

With a click of a key, from deep in my bed,
I ponder life's questions that dance in my head.
Why do we yawn? What makes the sun shine?
And why are there cats who think they divine?

In the search bar, I stumble and play,
Ask how to dance, or the best place to stay.
Finding the humor in life's little quirks,
As Google responds with its clever perks.

Do birds get bored? Can trees really sigh?
What is that sound when the squirrels fly by?
I type with a smile, enjoying the ride,
For grains of knowledge, my search is my guide.

Life's not just data, it's laughter and cheer,
Each question a treasure that brings me near.
So here's to the queries, so wild and so free,
Riding this wave of ridiculous glee.

The World at Our Fingertips

Here on my screen, the world comes alive,
With every quick tap, my thoughts start to jive.
From the wild to the wacky, there's always a way,
To learn if llamas want to join in the play.

Why do we snore? Is Bigfoot legit?
Can you train a goldfish to jump or to sit?
I scour the web for amusing delights,
While sipping my coffee, the morning ignites.

A click takes me places, both strange and sublime,
Finding odd facts that defy space and time.
With laughter as currency, in every search,
I build my own world, climbing knowledge's perch.

So let's raise a toast to this wondrous spree,
Exploring the cosmos through wit and esprit.
With the world at our fingertips, dreams come to play,
In this comical quest, we laugh all the way.

Gleaning Truth Through Code

In the depths of my search bar, I dive,
To find answers that help me survive.
How to boil water, or bake a pie,
A digital chef, oh me, oh my!

Counting calories, or training a dog,
Finding the space to unwind my fog.
What's the cure for a pesky cold?
Some tips from the web, all to behold!

Why do cats sit on keyboards all day?
Or the secret to making socks never stray.
From memes about life to a new shoe style,
The web knows it all, with a wink and a smile.

In every query, I find such delight,
Life's puzzles unraveled with a click and a light.
So here I remain, a curious geek,
In a world full of wonders, there's bliss to speak!

Echoes of Inquiry

Oh Google, my guide, with your vast repertoire,
Tell me the answer, open every door.
Why do birds sing, why does bread rise?
In the land of the online, I seek and I prize.

Questions flow freely like coffee from pots,
And the advice found can hit the right spots.
Can plants hear me talk, will they give me a sign?
I search for the wisdom one query at a time.

What's the secret to perfecting a pie?
Why does my phone think I'm always nearby?
In the echo of keys, my thoughts start to race,
Each search brings me closer to life's funny face.

As laughter ensues from each quirky find,
The absurdity blossoms, amusingly kind.
In this web of inquiry, so silly, so bright,
I chase all my wonders, from morning till night!

Filters of Reality

I type in my woes, and the screen starts to glow,
How to fix a hairdo? The secrets I know!
With every new filter, my selfies advance,
I'll look like a model, I'll take my chance!

The truth is out there, or so they say,
What's better than scrolling on a lazy day?
When did my pet learn to dance like that?
A viral sensation, or just a fat cat?

Finding out why my phone's always dead,
Or the best way to sleep on a cold, rainy bed.
A mix of the strange with the mundane and plain,
My searches unravel both joy and the pain.

Reality twists through the lens of my screen,
A whirlwind of facts, both clear and obscene.
So I click and I giggle, in my search I delight,
Filtering life through the pixels of light!

Sitemap of the Soul

Where do dreams go when they vanish and fade?
I type out my queries, my fears are displayed.
Are unicorns real? Can I summon a genie?
In this daunting dark, I'm feeling so teeny.

What's the best way to nap in my chair?
Or how to conquer the fridge without care?
Life is a maze, like a website's wide net,
With links to the strange, and I'm placing my bet.

How to adult, or how to make friends?
Each search feels like fun, but where does it end?
A sitemap of jests, my mind fills with glee,
Questions to ponder, just let it be free.

With every new search, I can laugh at the ride,
For the maps of my soul have no need to hide.
In this digital dance, I twirl and I sway,
Living and giggling through each funny foray!

The Algorithm of Immortality

A click away from living forever,
Let's find those answers, let's untether.
Can I transfer my mind to the cloud?
Or is that just a dream, too loud?

Eating kale and drinking green juice,
Hoping to find the magical juice.
How to live past one hundred years?
Maybe I'll ask while drowning my fears.

Search for youth tips, tips on staying fit,
Endless lists of what I must commit.
But sometimes I think, 'what's the cost?'
When all this searching, happiness lost?

In this vast web of endless queries,
I giggle at the thoughts that it carries.
For immortality is just a ploy,
To keep us clicking, chasing some joy.

Searching for Solace

In midnight hours when dreams run dry,
I search for answers, oh my oh my!
'How to find peace?' the query I type,
As the cat sprawls out, feeling quite ripe.

Binge-watch a show on how to chill,
Or dive deep in memes, that could do the thrill.
'Why does my life sometimes feel like spam?'
Maybe I just need a calming jam.

Find me a cosmo, or a guided breath,
Or just cat videos, to evade the stress.
Searching for solace through the screen's glow,
In this brave new world, I ebb and flow.

With every search, I find a new way,
To laugh at the chaos of life's ballet.
Behind each query, there's humor at play,
Finding solace, come what may.

Online Odyssey

I set sail on the sea of screens,
With pop-ups and links, and wild daydreams.
'How to cook pasta, or save a dime?'
My journey's a montage, bright, quite sublime.

The labyrinth of searches, both fun and bizarre,
Though the path is littered with ads from afar.
'Can I train my dog to do a backflip?'
Or just teach him to sit, that's a cool trip.

Each click an adventure, a quest of delight,
On this odyssey, I can drift through the night.
Let's Google my way to a tropical isle,
Where the internet greets me with a sunny smile.

Yet amid all the laughter and joy from the search,
I wonder if wisdom's still left to perch.
For a life well-lived can't just be a scroll,
But with every click, I'm still searching for soul.

The Questions We Never Ask

There's more to life than work and play,
But what are those queries we let slip away?
Why do pigeons strut as if they're elite?
And what's the best way to really cheat heat?

Do fish ever get thirsty, or need a break?
And how do we know if cake is a mistake?
Can you Google search for friendship's warm call?
Or is that too much for algorithms to haul?

I ponder the questions that tickle my brain,
Like 'why do socks vanish and never remain?'
In the whirl of thoughts, I'm giggling still,
With those silly questions, I'll chase every thrill.

So here's to the queries we cast to the void,
To the whimsical answers that we've all enjoyed.
For in this vast cosmos of search and text,
The funniest answers are what I'll index.

The Screen Door to the Soul

Click and type, a quest begun,
Searching for life, just having fun.
In pixels bright, we seek the truth,
Ice cream recipes and timeless youth.

Lost in tabs, I ponder fate,
What's my horoscope? Oh, it's late!
How to fold a fitted sheet,
Is the world flat? Oh, what a feat!

LOL and ROFL, a meme ignites,
Cat videos filling our nights.
Click, scroll, and we giggle away,
In cyberspace, we dance and play.

Yet behind the screen, a heart beats warm,
Seeking solace, safety from storm.
In every search, a flicker of soul,
Through this portal, we seek what's whole.

Questions That Light the Path.

Searching for snacks, pizza or fries?
How to ask for a raise, oh my!
Why do cats stare, what do they know?
Endless queries in this digital flow.

How to impress a date tonight?
Should I wear blue, or go with white?
Is chocolate healthy? Can it be so?
Questions pop up like grass in a row.

Where to find joy? Where to get gas?
Maps guide my way, as memories pass.
Can I train my dog to dance with flair?
Oh, the web knows—I just have to stare!

In every search, a light shines bright,
Silly, profound, from morning to night.
With clicks and laughs, we find our path,
In questions we trust, sparking our laugh.

Virtual Echoes

Echoes of laughter bounce off the screen,
Memes and puns, a digital sheen.
What's a good joke? Tell me, my friend,
In this virtual world, fun's never end.

Searching for wisdom, a quirky delight,
How to make pets look cute in the light?
What to watch next? My list is so long,
Dancing through searches, like dough to a song.

Did it really happen? Or am I misled?
Where do my thoughts go when I hit the bed?
Google, my oracle, with responses so swift,
Sharing my dreams with a humorous twist.

In the echoes of clicks, I feel so alive,
Tales and tricks that help me thrive.
With every query, a smile I find,
In this online chaos, so whimsically kind.

Digital Footprints

Footprints in pixels, a trail left behind,
Searching for wisdom, oh, how we find!
Where's the nearest taco truck?
Lost in the matrix, with just one click.

Recipes packed with extra zest,
How to nap better? A much-needed rest.
Is pineapple on pizza a culinary sin?
Daring debates make my head spin!

Where's the best coffee? What's trending now?
Fashion advice from a site I allow.
In these breadcrumbs, my thoughts intertwine,
Laughing at blunders, both yours and mine.

In this vast jungle of digital paths,
Adventures await, with giggles and laughs.
With every search, a new tale unfolds,
In our virtual socks, together we're bold.

The Librarian of Lost Questions

In the archives of clicks and taps,
The librarian laughs at our mishaps.
'What's the capital of Mars?' we ask,
As she adjusts her thick glasses, quite the task.

Forgotten recipes from dusty screens,
Returning to search for forgotten beans.
'Can I find my socks in this wild web?'
She chuckles softly, 'Just look under your bed!'

Instead of wisdom, we get pop-up ads,
For products we don't need; oh, how it drags!
'The meaning of life,' we type with glee,
She shrugs and says, 'Maybe just a cup of tea?'

In this digital realm of endless scrolls,
Attempting to fill in life's many holes.
With every search, a laugh is near,
For every lost nugget, a chuckle or cheer.

Wisps of Wonder in the Cyber Wilderness

Wandering through data, oh what a trip,
Losing my way with every click.
'How do you cook a cloud?' I ponder,
As the screen fades out, I start to wander.

A swath of wonders, memes and more,
Searching for wisdom behind the door.
'Are unicorns real?' my fingers fly,
The answer pops up, 'Only in the sky!'

Oh, the absurdity of endless quests,
To find the truth, and fail the tests.
'How tall is a giraffe in space?' I muse,
Type with glee, expecting to snooze.

In this wilderness where we all roam,
Seeking satisfaction, but feeling alone.
A click leads to laughter, that's no surprise,
For every search left unanswered, we rise.

Clicking Through the Cosmos

Fingers dance lightly on keys so bright,
'Can I order pizza that's out of sight?'
In the dark corners of cyberspace,
A craving hits, and I lose the race.

Planets whir by, I'm lost in the swirl,
Searching for facts in a digital whirl.
'Can you teach me to juggle with stars?'
I giggle and chuckle at my cosmic bars.

Days blend together like sticky notes,
Filling my mind with whimsical quotes.
'What's a good name for an alien pet?'
I dig and I wiggle, no answer yet!

With each click of the mouse, adventures ignite,
Endless questions float into the night.
From black holes to breakfast, each search a delight,
In this cosmic game, we laugh with sheer might.

Internet Riddles and the Human Search

Wrapped in riddles, a world so wide,
We chase the truth, the fun of the ride.
'Why is the sky so blue?' we query,
A thousand replies, yet none seem merry.

Every search starts with a curious mind,
Answering questions that are never aligned.
'Can toast really fly when it's burnt?' I muse,
While the internet snickers, it's what we choose.

In a sea of wisdom and viral dreams,
Each click reveals the wildest schemes.
'Why do cats sit on keyboards at night?'
The pages return with virtual light.

Through the web we wonder, a journey of glee,
Unraveling riddles that set minds free.
In this webbed labyrinth, side by side,
We giggle and ponder, oh what a ride!

A Search History of the Soul

In the quiet of the night, I type,
'How do I find my purpose?'
Yet, cat videos pop up,
And I'm lost in purring bliss.

Typed in 'how to be happy',
Got a recipe for pie.
Now I'm craving dessert,
Who needs philosophy?

I search for wisdom deep,
But find memes instead.
'Why are socks never a pair?'
These thoughts fill my head.

So I laugh and I scroll,
Life's cosmic joke unfolds,
As I hunt for the meaning,
In GIFs and cat folds.

Fragments of Wonder in the Web

Lost in a cyber maze,
I typed, 'Is Bigfoot real?'
But found a dog in a cape,
His powers? A squeaky heel.

'How to talk to aliens?'
And please, no more ads!
I end up in conspiracy,
While giggling like mad.

Google says, 'Try yoga!',
I'm flexible with snacks.
Yet searching for calmness,
Turns into Netflix hacks.

In a world of queries vast,
I learn where memes collide.
Each search a little journey,
With humor as my guide.

Typing Through the Maze of Memory

On my keyboard I ponder,
'Was it a dream or real?'
But suggestions fill the screen,
Of made-up meals to meal.

Each question leads to more,
'What's the secret to bliss?'
But I find a recipe,
For the perfect cheesy twist.

My mind drifts like a kite,
With queries soaring high.
'Life hacks for a better day?'
Or 'How to train a fly?'

In this digital realm,
Where moments seamlessly bend,
I find myself typing,
For fun, not just to transcend.

Breadcrumbs on a Digital Path

Click by click, I wander,
'How to be an ace?'
Google suggests a sandwich,
In a whimsy-like race.

I've searched 'How to meditate?',
Found a guide on tacos.
Each path leads to laughter,
As my stomach now growls.

'What's the meaning of life?'
Turns into 'Best cat trails.'
As I follow the breadcrumbs,
To where the humor prevails.

Through pixels and puns,
My queries dance like fire.
In this vast digital maze,
I type and never tire.

Parameters of Perception

Click, click, quirk of fate,
Typing fast, I can't be late.
Searching for the missing sock,
Found a cat that loves to rock.

Wonders fill the endless might,
Can I bake, and will it bite?
Recipes from realms obscure,
Can toast be made with just a door?

Lost in thoughts, where did I stray?
Google maps can save the day.
Lost my car, it's in the 'F'
For furious searches, it's my rep.

Be it facts or bacon tips,
In giggles, my curiosity flips.
What's the secret to a good meme?
In laughter's code, I find the theme.

Hints and Hypotheses

Why do pigeons walk like that?
Experts say, they just are fat.
I ponder deep, seeking insight,
Do they dream of pizza night?

Queries fly through virtual air,
How to curl my luscious hair?
Watch a video, two or three,
Then I ask, is hair still me?

Can I make a wish on toast?
My breakfast dreams, a joyful boast.
Jiffy recipes or long sautes,
All I need, Google parades.

Laughs abound in web's embrace,
Finding joy in this pixel place.
In a sea of bytes and hashtags,
I discover life through funny gags.

Coded Epiphanies

In bytes I find my closest friend,
Searching for that perfect blend.
How to use a blender right?
Avoiding splashes, what a fright!

Mysteries in the mundane found,
Is it chaos or is it sound?
What makes bread rise, who would know?
Let the geeks and nerds bestow!

Puns and memes all have a place,
How many dogs fit in this space?
A simple glance and I'm aglow,
With every click, the knowledge flows.

Random facts bring laughter's grace,
What's the deal with outer space?
I search for wisdom, crave a plight,
In Google's world, I find my light.

Meandering Through Metadata

In the web, I twist and turn,
Searching for all my concerns.
How to make a perfect pie,
Then wonder why do ovens lie?

With every page, my worries plead,
Can I plant a talking seed?
Answers come in bits and bytes,
Tangled truths in digital sights.

Lost in gags of the unknown,
Seeing life from a silly throne.
Can I train my pet to dance?
Just type away, give it a chance!

Humor flows like data streams,
In every quest, I find my dreams.
What a treasure, quirky and bold,
In laughter's arms, my heart is sold.

Reality in the Search Results

In the scroll of endless bars,
I seek what makes me laugh and cry.
A video cat in a fancy car,
Or how to bake a pie in the sky.

From memes that dance on digital spaces,
To lists of things I cannot afford,
I click through life like various faces,
Searching for joy I can't quite hoard.

Each query leads to rabbit holes,
Where wisdom plays hide and seek.
How to fix my plant with no souls,
Or the best way to perfect my squeak.

In the end, I just want to feel,
That humor's a click away, it seems.
With every search, my heart can heal,
In this vast web of silly dreams.

Through the Cyber Looking Glass

I typed the question, where's my shoe?
The answer's page turned into a show.
A rabbit ran, but where it flew,
Led me to a place I didn't know.

Frogs that sing and dance on screens,
Turn into job offers for kings.
In my quest for simple routines,
I find wild things life often brings.

Searching for lunch, I found my fate,
A recipe for tacos on toast.
Pandemonium on every plate,
With a side of laughter, I can boast.

Beyond the mirror, jokes unfold,
In pixels bright, the world's a mess.
I click to find treasures untold,
And giggle at my cyberspace quest.

The Digital Diaspora

In a land of emojis, I roam,
Searching for meaning with GIFs in hand.
Queries dart like bees to the foam,
Chasing answers across the land.

Why do socks vanish? Tell me more,
Am I alone in this endless race?
Click, click, clicking, I can't ignore,
The plight of my missing shoe lace.

With every scroll, wisdom unfolds,
Like a treasure found in the cloud.
In the digital chaos, life scolds,
Yet laughter blooms amongst the crowd.

On forums, I spill my light-hearted fears,
Will there be free food at the next meet?
In bytes and bits, I shed my tears,
Searching, always searching, for something sweet.

Finding Fragments in the Fog

I lost my keys somewhere online,
Help me search through the pixel haze.
A million tabs, a funny line,
Can bring my sanity back for days.

Query for lost socks adds to the game,
With the odds stacked like a giant hill.
A riddle in mist, I feel quite lame,
Yet search again brings a thrill.

With every glitch, laughter's around,
I find humor in the absurdity.
From random quests, joy is found,
In the silly slips of our digitality.

As I chase fragments, giggles arise,
Life becomes a quirky dance.
In this chaotic web of lies,
Every search feels like a funny chance.

Inquiries Beneath the Surface Screen

Endless questions, one by one,
Typing queries, oh what fun!
'Can cats dance? Do fish sing?'
The knowledge grows, let laughter ring!

In the depths of the web, I dive,
Seeking answers, feeling alive.
'Why do socks vanish in the wash?'
Links to wisdom, a digital nosh!

With each click, more mysteries hide,
A rabbit hole, my thoughts collide.
'Is cereal a soup?' I ponder,
Without answers, I sit and wander.

As I scroll through memes and lore,
Each odd fact opens another door.
Life's a riddle, a playful tease,
Solving it all, with giggles, please!

The Quest for Meaning in a Click

In cyberspace, I roam so wide,
With queries dancing by my side.
'Why do we park on driveways?'
My giggles echo in playful phase!

I seek the truth with a Googling grin,
'How do you fold a fitted sheet, again?'
All life's puzzles at my command,
From tacos to time, it's all so grand!

Each search reveals a little more,
Awkward facts I can't ignore.
'Is it normal to talk to pets?'
These digital wonders set no regrets.

I squash my fears with every fetch,
'Why does my cat think I'm a wretch?'
In this web of questions and cheer,
Discovery finds me year after year!

Online Reflections of the Mind

With a whisk of a finger, I inquire,
'Can I teach my goldfish to inspire?'
The answers come, both silly and bright,
Like glittering stars in the deep night.

'What's the secret to perfect fries?'
Search results bring laughter, no surprise.
I sift through tips, the good and the bad,
For every search, there's a laugh to be had!

Scrolling memes, I seek and learn,
'Why do we yawn? Is it just a turn?'
Such quirky wonders weave through my thought,
In this rich tapestry, joy is sought!

The digital world is my charming stage,
Where every query could spark a new page.
Life's enigmas, in bytes, they gleam,
In each search, I uncover a dream!

Puzzles Lurking in Search Bars

'Why do we say 'break a leg'?
Does it mean something? That's my peg!
To the great search engine, I throw my plea,
For answers wrapped in mystery!

Scrolling past, I find delight,
'How do you get rid of grape spite?'
Such oddball queries bring forth a smile,
It's the beauty of surfing every so while.

From random facts to recipes fit,
Every click sparks a humorous split.
'Can I microwave a metal spoon?'
It's a dance with answers that keep me in tune!

With each search, I chuckle and grin,
Seeking wisdom from outside in.
Life's a puzzle made of jest,
In the world of clicks, I'm truly blessed!

Digital Musings

In the depths of my screen I dwell,
Typing questions, casting my spell.
'Why is the sky blue?' I inquire,
Google knows more than I ever could desire.

With each click, a new path unfurls,
From cats on skateboards to time-traveling girls.
'How to cook pasta?' is a daily plight,
But it's often takeout that wins the night.

I spill coffee, a stream of dread,
Typing 'Can I revive my phone from the dead?'
It's amazing what wisdom a search can provide,
Between memes and recipes, my thoughts coincide.

Life's a puzzle, a humorous quest,
In the world of keywords, I'm truly blessed.
With each phrase I toss into the void,
I find my answers, and chaos destroyed.

Navigating Through Noise

In a sea of data, it's hard to breathe,
Queries float by as I grasp and weave.
'What's that song stuck in my head?' I plead,
Auto-suggestions become my lifeline, indeed.

'How to adult?' is a search I regret,
Finding answers that only create more debt.
'Can dogs wear pants?' ignites my delight,
Each answer just fuels my endless night.

The search bar's filled with my quirky needs,
From plant care to fashion, my mind feeds.
'What's the meaning of life?' twists my mood,
But 'how to bake cookies?' puts me in food.

Amongst all the data, I sift and scroll,
Trying to find what makes me whole.
With laughter and confusion, I plow right through,
In the web's wacky world, my soul will renew.

Shadows in the Search Bar

Late-night browsing, screen's glowing bright,
Questions unending, lost in the light.
'Why do I feel like a potato?' I muse,
As a million results turn my brain into blues.

Each click is a journey, a twist in my fate,
Google's my guide, at an uncaring rate.
'How to dance like nobody's watching?' I grin,
While searching for 'quirky' is where I'll begin.

In the shadows of queries, I find my fun,
From bizarre DIYs to finding a pun.
'Why does my cat stare?' brings me some cheer,
As my computer chuckles, I've nothing to fear.

Through the web of wonders, I laugh and play,
In each search, absurdity rules the day.
Unraveling the depths of what makes me tick,
With humor and insight, life's a clever trick.

The Search for Identity

Who am I really? I type in dismay,
Tangled in questions that lead me astray.
'What's my spirit animal?' I start to explore,
Before long, I'm lost in a quiz once more.

'How to reinvent myself?' echoes my plea,
Only to find I'm just searching for me.
'Can I wear socks with sandals?' is pure gold,
A new fashion trend, daring and bold!

Turning the pages of answers unread,
Am I a dreamer, or stuck in my bed?
'Help, I'm confused!' I exclaim in despair,
Yet Google responds: 'You're fully aware!'

From questions absurd to wisdom so bright,
I grapple with answers, both wrong and right.
With a search engine's help, I'll find my crest,
In this wild game of life, I'll figure the rest.

Echoes of Thoughts in a Search Field

Clicking through tabs of my day,
Hoping for answers that tease and play.
A query or two, and then I sigh,
"How to cook pasta?" Just tell me why!

The cat on the keyboard, a helpful muse,
"How to find lost socks?" I'm bound to lose.
A rabbit hole beckons with memes and gifs,
And suddenly, I've forgotten my lists.

Diagnosis sought through the screen's bright glow,
"Is my cough normal?" Let's take it slow.
The wisdom of the web, a quirky beast,
I find more questions than answers, at least!

A simple life hack becomes a grand quest,
"Best way to nap?" I just need some rest.
With every search, a new laugh I find,
The joy of the digital, oh so kind!

The Diary of Digital Dreams

In pixels and posts, I share my plight,
"How to dance like no one's watching tonight?"
A dance move followed by puppy memes,
Clicking through channels of whimsical dreams.

I write my memoir in cookies and cache,
"How to impress?" A dash and a flash.
Spilling my secrets, I type in a rush,
"How to tie shoelaces?" Old tricks in a hush.

My digital diary's a curious blend,
With life hacks and recipes, all without end.
"How to eat healthy?" The struggle is real,
Those late-night snack cravings have mass appeal.

I scroll and I giggle, there's more to explore,
"How to get rich?" Well, that's just folklore.
In the diary of clicks, wisdom reigns true,
But mostly it's laughter when searching for clues!

Hints of Humanity in Hyperlinks

In a world of links, I wander so wide,
"How to be funny?" A waste of my pride.
In viral sensations, we lose track of time,
With cat videos playing, all feeling sublime.

"How to clean wisely?" A chore I detest,
Yet here comes a meme, it's all for the jest.
Life's messy and wild, but oh what a treat,
In hyperlinks lay the tales bittersweet.

A search for connection, I type and I press,
"Why do I procrastinate?" Just one more guess.
I navigate moments with laughter as guide,
Amongst all the chaos, joy's not to hide.

With questions aplenty, I'm losing my wits,
"How to have fun with just a few clicks?"
Humanity shines in the clicks on the screen,
As laughter and wisdom blend in between!

Seeking Silence in a Noisy World

In a world full of chirps, I'm hunting for peace,
"How to meditate?" Just give me some grease.
With earbuds in, I block out the hum,
As I scroll for answers, feeling all dumb.

The search bar whispers, a soft lullaby,
"How to find calm?" I look to the sky.
Between the chaos, I seek out a break,
With funny memes drinking my morning shake.

Questions keep coming like waves on a shore,
"How to stop thinking?" Oh, what a chore.
Yet laughter is gold in this buzzing bazaar,
As I find humor beneath every star.

I'm seeking that silence, in pixels so bright,
"How to feel centered?" An endless delight.
But through all the noise, there's a chuckle to share,
Life's a search party; to you, I declare!

Search Bar Reflections

Typing my woes, a click and a glow,
Answers appear like stars in a row.
What should I wear, what's the best snack?
Oh, how I wish there was no going back!

Getting advice from strangers online,
Is this the part where I draw the line?
How to impress with just a few words,
Life's little mysteries, solved by the nerds!

From baking a cake to fixing my car,
These searches make me feel like a star.
A library of questions, archives of dreams,
All neatly organized in pixelated streams!

So here I sit, with a chuckle and grin,
Googling my way through thick and thin.
In this tangled web, I take my stand,
Searching for meaning with a click of my hand!

The Archives of Experience

Memories saved in the cloud above,
Mistakes and victories, all things we love.
How to cook pasta? How to dance right?
Each search reveals a new path in sight.

Browsing through life like a digital book,
Finding solutions in each little nook.
Can you believe all the things that I've tried?
With help from the web, I'm along for the ride!

From awkward first dates to fixing my hair,
Algorithms guiding me everywhere.
I laugh at my queries, they're silly, it's true,
But hey, it beats stressing with nothing to do!

In the archives of experience, I often lose track,
Of random searches leading me back.
To moments that shape my peculiar life,
A search engine tool in this digital strife!

Connections in Cyberspace

A friend requests help with a sneeze,
Google suggests ten ways to appease.
We laugh through the screens, share gifs and memes,
In cyberspace life, we're living our dreams!

How to pull a prank? Oh, what a delight,
YouTube tutorials make everything right.
From random recipes to great travel spots,
The web is a playground connecting the dots!

Swipe left or right, in love I'm a geek,
Searching for partners, adventure I seek.
Each click is a gamble, a roll of the dice,
In this digital dance, there's always a spice!

Through tangled connections, I find my own way,
Each search leads to laughter from day into day.
In this cyberspace chaos, I've found my own grace,
Building funny connections in our vast interface!

Data Dreams

Pillow thoughts filled with ones and with zeros,
Searching for truth, I'm my own superhero.
How to find love? Is pineapple a crime?
In data dreams drifting, I'm lost in the rhyme.

My wish list is long, from gadgets to snacks,
Life's little questions are part of the tracks.
When boredom strikes, I just type and I click,
Each result brings a smile, or sometimes a trick!

Late night queries stir up playful delight,
Like "How to become a cat whisperer overnight?"
In a world full of wonders, I'm never alone,
Each search just a giggle, a dance on its own.

So here's to the questions that keep us awake,
The funny discoveries, the searches we make.
In these data dreams, we unravel the scheme,
Life's quirky adventures, just part of the meme!

Navigating the Unknown

In the depths of the web, I dive and I roam,
Searching for answers, will I find my way home?
From cat memes to recipes, oh what a sight,
Lost in the pixels, it feels just so right.

Type in my symptoms, oh what could it be?
A simple cold or the plague, I decree!
Dr. Google is wise, knows all of my woes,
Yet somehow I'm sure, it's just allergies' throes.

The map of my thoughts, all laid out in clicks,
A trail of my questions, a series of tricks.
From "How to cook pasta?" to "How to unwind?"
Each search leads to laughter, and knowledge I find.

So here's to the quest, with humor we log,
Navigating life through the internet fog.
Every whim, every whim, fuels my curious fire,
In this wacky world, I could never tire.

The Curiosity Algorithm

I googled my crush, what's their star sign please?
The link led to fortune, and a few heartache keys.
Clicking 'next' like a rat in a maze,
Searching for love through a digital haze.

What's the best pizza, or how to look cool?
The web knows it all, it's an infinite school.
From "Is my dog mad?" to "How to break dance?",
Each query's a step in the search engine's trance.

How do I start a band? Who needs a plan?
Whoa, a guide for it all, "Become a rockman!"
Trolling through wisdom, humor does bloom,
With just one more click, I'll escape this gloom.

So, here I sit typing, deep into the night,
Finding that info makes everything right.
An adventure online, a rollercoaster ride,
With memes, laughs, and chats as my trusty guide.

Clicks and Whispers

In the quiet of night, I type with delight,
What's the meaning of dreams? I search for the light.
From UFOs to cupcakes, the rabbit hole spins,
With each little click, come the laughter and grins.

Searching for wisdom, but all I find's fun,
How to train my cat? Or how to shoot sun?
The whispers of sages echo through my head,
Yet I follow the jokes instead of the dread.

Oh Google, my friend, you know too much indeed,
From "Best dad jokes!" to "What's wrong with my seed?"

Each query a puzzle, a dance in the dark,
Creating my path, a quirky little spark.

So here's to the searches, the laughs that they bring,
In the world of the web, we're all searching kings.
With humor our compass, we wander as one,
In this vast digital realm, let the searches be fun!

The Digital Diary

Today I lost socks, where do they all go?
A quest to uncover, I'll search high and low.
What wear to the party? Or how to make cake?
My digital diary knows all of my takes.

Inquiring about life hacks, I stumble and trip,
"No egg? Just a meme!" It gives love a grip.
Tips on great selfies, what's the best angle?
All of my friends, with my photos they dangle.

What's the worst dad joke? Oh, let's find out more,
With punchlines and puns, laughter's in store.
Click, click, click—each revelation a gem,
I stitch them together, a digital hymn.

Tomorrow's agenda, I'll write down the whim,
This online journal, full of laughs on a whim.
Each search an adventure, with joy and delight,
In this silly old world, it all feels just right.

Whispers of Wisdom in an Inbox

Each day a new cat meme found,
The wisdom of ages, all around.
Clicking 'reply' like a true sage,
In this inbox, we earn our wage.

A sale on socks caught my eye,
Do I need them? Oh well, why not try?
Between the spam and the daily grind,
Truth and laughter, we oft find.

Learning to cook? Just one more click,
That recipe for a magical trick.
A dash of humor, a pinch of fun,
The art of survival, for everyone.

So here's to the wisdom we collect,
From corridors digital, we reflect.
In an inbox where giggles reside,
A treasure trove we must not hide.

The Virtual Footprints of Us

With every click, a path we lay,
Through memes and tweets, we find our way.
Virtual footprints all around,
In the grid of pixels, we are bound.

'Where's the best taco?' we query loud,
Maps and reviews, we're so proud.
A dance with algorithms, oh so sly,
Finding joy as we scroll by.

Pictures of dinners, trips, and fun,
All shared online, they weigh a ton.
Laughter echoes in every like,
A digital hug, a friendly spike.

As we surf the waves of electric sea,
We find ourselves, you and me.
In the vastness, we take a stand,
Virtual footprints, hand in hand.

Data Streams and Dreaming Thoughts

In streams of data, my mind can roam,
Each notification feels like home.
Searching 'how to nap like a pro',
A skill we all secretly wish to know.

Cats in boxes, why do they fit?
A profound question, I must admit.
Scrolling through memes, for hours I go,
Finding joy in the highs and the low.

Facetime to friends who are far away,
'How to bake bread?' is the game we play.
With every search, a new delight,
In this symphony of bytes, we take flight.

Data streams flow while dreaming we snore,
Each query a reason to laugh and explore.
In the ocean of knowledge, we take a dive,
Making sense of all this, we thrive.

Curated Lives in a Browser

In a world where filters reign supreme,
Curated lives fulfill a dream.
With each click, a life designed,
Perfection caught, so well aligned.

Scrolling through travel, food, and art,
Every profile a work of heart.
Yet behind the gloss, we hold our truths,
In the digital mess, we hide our goofs.

'How to live better?' the search bar shines,
Witty quotes wrapped in digital vines.
But beneath the laughter, what do we see?
Just a mirror reflecting you and me.

So laugh at the chaos, embrace the grind,
In this browser world, seek and find.
Curated lives can be so sweet,
Yet it's our quirky selves that make us complete.

Enigmas of the Digital Age

Clicking keys in the quiet night,
Secrets hide just out of sight.
What's that rash? Do I have a curse?
The answers leave me feeling worse.

Why does my cat stare so intently?
Is it wisdom, or simply empty?
Do aliens watch me from the sky?
Or am I just living a big lie?

How to cook rice without a fuss?
Do I need a pot or can I trust?
Instructions dance in digital mirth,
But mine still somehow taste like dirt.

I seek my soulmate in ones and zeroes,
They must exist, my digital heroes!
How long will I search for that perfect match?
Or is this just a clever prank, a glitchy batch?

Queries in the Quiet Hours

Late at night with just my screen,
I ponder all the things I've seen.
Why do socks vanish without a trace?
Did they join a secret hiding place?

Can I teach my dog to use the phone?
Will he call me when I'm alone?
How to break up with my lazy chair?
It doesn't listen, it just doesn't care.

Why is pizza my favorite food?
Is it the cheese, or simply mood?
How many toppings are too many?
Each click leaves my heart a bit heavy.

Searching for answers as I recline,
Life's quirky puzzles make me pine.
Do I need to Google my own name?
Or is it best to stay safe in my game?

Searching the Echoes of Existence

In the depths of the midnight glow,
Questions bubble up like dough.
What's the meaning of that strange dream?
Am I the star or just a meme?

Why is my fridge always empty?
Did I eat it all, or's it just my plea?
How can I bake a fluffy soufflé?
Or will it deflate and run away?

Can my goldfish understand my woes?
Does he judge me? Who really knows?
Why do I never remember my password?
In this maze, I feel like a coward.

Every search leads to another round,
A carousel of joy I've found.
Is it brilliant or just plain absurd?
In this digital life, have I lost my word?

The Infinite Scroll of Being

Scrolling depths that never cease,
Curiosity fueled by digital grease.
Why do plants always seem to die?
Is it a curse or just a lie?

Why can't I find the remote control?
It's vanished, swallowed by the whole.
How do I tame this crazy stress?
Can I Google a life coach's address?

Am I alone in this quirky quest?
Or is everyone on a similar test?
What's the secret to a perfect selfie?
Or is it just filters that help me?

Questions zipping like a buzzing fly,
Each click could lead to the reason why.
Living in pixels, I seek and peek,
For wisdom lies where the browsers leak.

A Journey of Keywords

In the realm of bytes and bits,
Searching for meaning in digital kinks.
"How to bake a cake?" it admits,
While I ponder existence in sync.

Google knows when I can't sleep,
"Symptoms of overthinking," it shows.
I laugh as my secrets I keep,
In this vast web where the data flows.

What makes us tick is quite absurd,
"How to tie a tie" on my screen.
For wisdom wrapped in every word,
I navigate this quirky machine.

Inquiries lead to hope and jest,
"What's the best cat video?" I plea.
As joy appears, so feels the quest,
In my browser, I find a spree.

Webs of Wonderment

Fingers dance on keys like stars,
Searching for joys or maybe woes.
"How to fix a broken heart?"
Oh, the thrill of what each search knows!

Through hyperlinks, I laugh and weep,
"Best ways to tell a dad joke!"
As endless threads around me creep,
Life's absurdity, no need to provoke.

Life's puzzles wrapped in HTML,
With memes and gifs as guides and jest.
Unlocking mysteries, oh so swell,
Internet wisdom is quite the quest.

With every click, a new delight,
"How to nap like a pro?" I muse.
Giggling at screens deep into the night,
In this web, we choose to cruise.

The Language of Longing

In a box of queries, I confide,
"Best ice cream flavors to try this summer?"
Wishing for sweetness, a joyful ride,
I laugh at my search, not a bummer.

"How to impress on a first date?"
Oh, the pressure that follows the clicks!
Endless advice, I contemplate,
Can charm really come from quick tricks?

On rabbit holes I whirl and spin,
"How to find the meaning of life?"
Each search reveals secrets within,
Although what I find may cause strife.

In the archives of wisdom I dwell,
"Why does my cat stare at me?"
In every whim, there's truth to tell,
In this funny quest, I feel free.

Pasting Pieces of Life

Copy and paste, that's how it goes,
"How to live without your phone?"
With each search, my laughter grows,
In these moments, I feel less alone.

Endless tabs open, bright and bold,
"How to tell if my food's gone bad?"
Life's simple truths in digital gold,
I chuckle at quirks, never sad.

Searching for answers, wisdom unfurls,
"Crazy cat fails" turns to chuckles galore.
In this chaos, a spark of pearls,
Each click a surprise, always wanting more.

Fragments of life in pixels and bytes,
"How to dance with no sense of beat?"
For joy in the silly, my spirit ignites,
In the search of the strange, I always feel neat.

www.ingramcontent.com/pod-product-compliance
Lightning Source LLC
Chambersburg PA
CBHW072147200426
43209CB00051B/826